MW01248123

A World in Which

Also by J. L. Conrad

A Cartography of Birds

Recovery (chapbook)
Not If But When (chapbook)
Species of Light (chapbook)

A World in Which

J. L. Conrad

Terrapin Books

Terrapin Books
4 Midvale Avenue
West Caldwell, NJ 07006

www.terrapinbooks.com

ISBN: 978-1-947896-73-4
Library of Congress Control Number: 2023952531

First Edition

Cover art by Amy Salomone
My Heart Beats with Nature
digital collage
www.formsmostbeautiful.com

Cover design by Diane Lockward

for my family,
chosen and inherited

Contents

Let this darkness be a bell tower
and you the bell. As you ring,
what batters you becomes your strength.

—Rainer Maria Rilke

1.

In Which I Try to Bring Back the Dead

It's a question of loss. Each afternoon I phone
from the glass booth beside the ocean, wind
driving air through the door cracks, sky flung haphazard.
Each night we enter the casino, taking our chances,
traveling the long corridors of lit stars. When it's clear
something else must be done, we remove
our names from the waiting list. Wearing bracelets
fashioned from spoons, we approach the truth
tree seeking to open the question, to settle
our differences. Later, as we eat breakfast, flocks
of nightingales cloud the air. There's no coffee to be found
for miles, and all signs point to walking: jaunty figures,
leaping deer, an air of yellow danger. A sense that
we might arrive at any one of our pasts is brewing.
Because we no longer need our bodies, we've
sent them packing. I try to name this grief. The day
holds thick as feathers. Your voice hums without breaking.

House Above the Bottomlands

The vegetal undertones of this new season.
This year's crop of bones
come up from the river's bed.

Joints worn as if long
put to use. A scatter marked
with white flags.

From the bluff it is possible
to glimpse birds
from above, sense their passage.

Grief darkens nightly.
What we find, we gather.
Unbranch and surface.

The space requires
one to settle into it, but one
is not yet comfortable here.

Landscape stitched to itself, this
window to the next.
The highway's ragged breath.

I have harbored you and then some.
As a hipbone pivots in its socket:
perfectly, with no ridges

to disturb its transit.
Traffic continues to churn, but
nothing moves except

the small fans of leaves
thrown out by the oak, prodigal tree.
Grief settles and makes a home.

Wings banked, all at once.
Rain with its clothing, its vascular ebb.
The subterfuge of this in-between.

This spark and hum.

Meanwhile

My dreams inscribe for me a world in which. And when the box arrives, it holds three blessings for the new home in which we are only sometimes married to each other. Where the cats stare into vents waiting for the dragon to start breathing. As if that weren't enough, the maples detach one leaf after another, which land with soft pops on the roof. I make plans for travel, then discard them. Book flights I do not take.

*　*　*

A chill day caught in the forceps of winter. The word *unimpeded* as in *the wind blew from the lake*. Water's teeth cutting into the shore. By accomplishing something I mean I have fixed the sink. Surely you didn't intend. I wear a black coat to solve my troubles. Skin betrays the eyes, and the long glint of your wanting does, as they say, no good.

*　*　*

The moon lifts light from the neighborhood. Air sends its warning, the sound of trains running all night along the backs of houses. Inside, arms lie alongside bodies of the already-known. Doors open to the east and west. Longings prefaced with—I'm at that age when. I think to *stave off*, to *save*, even. Never turn a clock backward you tell me.

* * *

I apply for entry to my own best life. Across the city, homes stand vacant: no windows lit, no shadows proceeding after feet. Birds assemble in formation, readying for some journey or another. Where they are headed I can't really say. We make them homes of our hands, offer bones as if in supplication.

* * *

Every day I watch our house from across the street. What looks like blood mars the bus stop wall. The secret to living this long is: a shield of luck worn around the body. Our names appear on the mail as if. This time when it slips through the flap, there's no going back. And yet I do not wish to disturb the starlings. The fact is, I don't even know what I'm homesick for.

In Which Our Best-Laid Plans
Come to Nothing

When the news broke, we found ourselves
stranded, though we'd drawn the escape routes
meticulously on our map: red for outbound lanes,
all options open. The transistor reported that
upwards of fifty animals had escaped the zoo
and were making their way down the boardwalk.
Someone observed the African Grey parrot, who
can live nearly as long as a person, winging his way
out to sea past the crabcakes and the iced gelato,
most of us clumped under umbrellas, our supply
of sunscreen all but exhausted. A pair of zebras
has taken up residence on the dunes. I can no longer
find my striped hat. It seems the sea has swallowed
it whole. Pack lightly, the guidebook advised.
Had we known we'd still be here lingering among
the salt-soaked books, the mailboxes knocked off-kilter
by the last big storm and the sign proclaiming
"Grand Open" on the new hotel, we would have
dismantled the stage set sooner, admitted our failings.
As it is, we can't boast about our preparations.

Miracle Town

in which we embrace the evidence

At first it seemed like a fluke: the skin not healing. The abraded knee the same weeks later, the finger onto which the knife slipped still wearing its flap. Then, when the accident at the corner of Pine and Venezuela made it clear this was to be our condition, we began keeping our children indoors, counting our losses. Someone soon invented a lightweight protective suit that provided the illusion we might be able to resume our late-night rounds of lawn darts, the skiing and skateboarding, the raking of leaves. Yet the suits were hot and, as became clear, susceptible to intrusions. Years passed. What we perceived as beautiful changed. Now, few remember when skin knit itself back together, leaving a seam, sure, but sealing off the self. Our histories of trauma etched into our bodies, open doors through which the world enters. Just now, the girl onstage in the spotlight recites a tale about a severed head, still singing.

A Dangerous Time, These Hours
in the Night

In the maple outside,
paired crows

squawk through

rain-wracked sky a bit frayed
at the edges then

batten down the hatches
and keep going.

In our apartment, the cat
staggers loose circles

on the living

room rug. Head off-
kilter, eyes shaking like marbles.

Body pitched over as if on deck.

Then crouched
underchaired

in the corner. We watch
shaken from sleep

by the crash of the falling.
We've called for help.

Minutes pass and then some.

Was it the blue-tailed lizard?
The chips of paint?

The meeting of skull with floorboards?

The phone says *disorder*
says *wait*.

This is *ataxia*. This is *nystagmus*.

The sky's clouds
are God's fingers. Like gray logs.

The light flank of morning
showing through.

I can't tell the difference between
desire and *design*.

The lake distinct and glass-faced.

Did the rain intend
this blind beating of leaves?

Skin-shivered
morning, wind-headed sky riddling

the screen. Off in the distance, zoobirds
mumble and disperse.

You whisper *there is*
a change.

On Edge as if Breaking

The moon thrusts its back above
a horizon line of trees laid low to earth—

Along the fence ahead, a lone deer stands,
spot-frozen and looking to leap into
the headlights' web that maps our way

onto the scattered snow-stars
of a smaller road, white lines curving north—

past a semi-trailer parked, "Fresh Produce"
set in red on its side—and arrows

to show the way. Love, I do not speak
of these, saying only, "I am sad
tonight," but not why when you ask.

A thousand times your face, and hands: rivers
have passed; I would not hurt you.

What I wish now, eight years out
from such beginnings is the stillness, wind-

opened and swept until even engines seem unmade,
slipping into what has always been—
sky, earth, the skim of frost on Queen Anne's

lace, and how that flower, stem-split, each half
planted in a dish of colored water, turns

half-red, half-blue in its fragility, perched
atop two glasses on the kitchen sill.

Postdrome

If this were the Before Time, then
you would have stayed with me.

Instead, I lie settled on
this bed tilted carefully so I am

not quite upright, not quite
reclining either. It is awkward, as is

this hospital gown they have me wearing.
Outside, snow hunches its way

toward the horizon. It's almost
the shortest day, or the longest night,

whichever way you would have it,
and which I say in order to locate

ourselves in this moment where
what I want to say is how,

this morning, when I read of
the chariots of fire and the whirlwind

descending, this blended with
the thundering hooves of my heart

as I lay on the kitchen floor,
the dogs barking in the next room

and rightfully so. Flecked salt
studs the sidewalk beyond the doors

like stars in the night sky where
scientists sought out the darkest patch

to be found, trained the telescope on it
for ten days and came back with

an image pocked not with constellations
but *galaxies*, two hundred sixty-five

thousand of them, an inestimable number.
And here spins our small home

on the outskirts of the universe,
some backwater really, where

days pass in a quick slurry,
months lost to a map with no compass.

Backdropped by sky, the red crane tilts
at cross-purposes, much like

our son, when asked to describe
the inkblot, saw llamas

sprinting from a burning barn
in opposite directions, a person with

a hole through them on the next card.
And here you are now, the car wearing

its white cap of snow, hurling itself
ever closer to where I lie waiting.

Heart Land

It is time for tea bags on the eyes.
A budding of anxiety, its roots and branches.

They never forewarn you about this shift.
I'm going to tell you how it works.

The last stand of trees along the horizon.
The parcel soon to be sold.

Snow eases its way through the fence.
Wind eats away at the ridgelines.

The car skids into the other car.
Two women climb out and face one another.

Count the ways the world should not exist.
We should give our possessions away.

Are you preppers? we are asked over and over.
People admire the rows of canned beans gleaming.

The moons of peaches glistening in the half light.
No, we say, these just keep showing up.

Let's not forget how life moved inside the body.
The paper at the heart of the fortune-teller.

The god who sits with you in darkness.
The god who will not leave your side.

The yews at least five decades in the making.
Limbs grown to our second-story windows.

Birds eat their way through the storehouse.
We place peppermint along the back sill.

Clumped cedars keep the road swathed in ice.
Snow fastened to one side of the trunks.

Still, love keeps unfolding.
The soft arm of your flannel shirt.

Flood, August

We have chosen a course
in which all of the answers are true:

a voice coming home to roost,

a light that turns on as if by
magic as night approaches.

Soft leaves pummeled by rain.

The piano travels over miles
of flooded roads to reach us.

This year, no peaches to wash.

Music running in the background
settles the nerves. At first

when the water begins to rise

people watch with curiosity, even
festivity, standing on the bridge

overlooking the river, or rather

the low-lying lake overtaking
the street next to its

bank of red-brick apartments.

We'd never thought to ask
what happens in a hundred-

year storm. We like to put

a human face on it.
How long do we have?

One answer: *longer than you think.*

Miracle Town

in which everything is cast aside

We choose, for instance, to take off our skins. Our bones
sheltering the soft animals of our organs. In the white
light of a winter moon, we parade together, bandying
about. Some carry flags. Others have stitched small
triangles of cloth together to form a banner. A word that
comes to mind is *festoon*. Another is *shimmy*. We make our
way out not knowing the way back. Together the bones of
our feet chatter. The city a long knife lying between two
blue eyes. The city a bridge we take toward an after in
which we will have learned, as it turns out, nothing. Wind
blows itself out against our foreheads. Flags flap on their
slender poles. The moon like a coin on the lid of each
closed eye.

By the Gazelles

I do not know which to prefer,
The beauty of inflections
Or the beauty of innuendoes.
                    —Wallace Stevens

Fingertips burn yellow—
invisible traces cross arms, the brim
of eyebrows.

Morning given to us
in sheets of light.

The spoked pine outside the window—
Cezanne's tree, you name it—
sifts a layer of sun.

I name the space next to me: *yours*.

What I remember: fingers' weight,
the skin's topography,
its alluvial plains.

The room diffuse with shadow,
a faintness. Refresh me
with pomegranates.

As one learns the chiaroscuro
of touch in night's silvered fields.
Unhinged from gravity—

after days of solstice,
of sweetness and collapse,

a concavity under cheekbones,
a voice like birds.

I searched and did not find.

The gatekeepers asked
why I wore this body.

I did not know how
to answer.

2.

Brother André's Heart, Montreal

In 1973, the heart gone, pilgrims
climb the stairs on knees to eye

the heartless man in his hollow chamber.
Memory's plumbline laid from there to here

on limestone. The mountain around which the city.
Yes, I remember. A new opening

through which the body remade itself.
Rocks knocked from mountainsides

brought here to bear weight upward until
even the impression of weight lifts off into

the recessed darkness pooled beneath the roof.
We stand in the votive chapel six days married.

A bank of candles: whipstitch of lights
sealing the wound. Columns bristle

with rows of crutches. We do not yet know
how bodies cave, how bones surface. We take

no pictures. No, that's not true.
We take two: one into the washed-out summer

sky. Me wearing sunglasses, the carved
angel rising behind my shoulder. And another

on surfacing from the crypt, sun breaking
into pieces, rimming each edge with light.

See how clouds cut into the sky.
See how the geese are black slashes

unstitching the firmament. Beyond
the open door, the heart lies suspended

in a jar, bathed in a red heatlamped glow.
The papers reported it found

in an empty apartment locked in a box
inside another box. How they must

have wrenched it from the body.
You've remembered it wrong

all these years: the jagged undoing,
snipping each stitch so the wound gapes open

again. Today, pilgrims file past the vault
in silence: my body parched, yours

stationed there beside me,
on the near side of desire. Holy water laid

between us. In what voice do I
call out? A brittle light, hearts sundered.

We can't be blamed if things come apart.
We can scarcely be accused of theft. What we take

we take from each other. Our dreams wearing horns
like sacrificial rams. We know in our bones,

which is to say our deepest selves, the world
thrown open, the veil torn, seeded fields ungrown

at last. It falls to us to shovel dirt over the flames.
Sometimes, they say, the heart still beats.

We did not ask for this. The one day a year
wine becomes unsettled, remembering.

Annunciation

The elm's last leaves are falling
still: Christmas and my father
at the window shooting starlings

as if they are more than nuisances:
instead, messengers that, left
unchecked, might shatter

our best conventions, rend
our lives thread by thread. Breath's
plume is a warning: blank air

thin enough to fracture, a dropped
seed would send hairline cracks
down the wild cherry's trunk,

split invisible seams. Ice crackles
in the feeders, on leaves, in
lungs. The gun's slick metal keeps

its implacable horizontal: no report,
just shot sun startling eyes, wings
rising in a black flurry, bird-

marked sky overhead: brief reprieve.

In the Midst of Reading Ammons

Bird beak and tree tether:
crusts of boulders hold to ground,
folds of soil clinging roots

into themselves. O improbable
essences, bear me to ground—
shape the unaskable

intransigence into birches, or ash
trees, whose branches (brittle)
even now are crumbling

making earth more
than it was, the bodies borne
changing back into new

growth, boulders'
rock spines caving,
letting in the light last.

In Which We Get Bogged
Down in Inessentials

I'd been meaning to get rid of it all: the empty
dresses, shoes meant for dancing on a single occasion,
the endless procession of books. The half-moon inches
its way overhead. *It's broken,* the child says. *When I get bigger,
I'll fix it.* I never promised my heart would be easy
to carry. Thin metal bands bisect the city, slicing
off one end from the other. Someone has stolen
the canaries, the ones meant to show danger in each
sealed room. Trees wait in their armor. Everything is beginning
to conspire against us, the fine machinery of our bodies
giving way, the soup churning under its skin.
I want you to know that today I'll be taking
the pie-in-the-sky approach despite winter's jaw snapping.
We sell the furniture out from under ourselves.
In the midst of it all, your heart never stops beating.

Tivoli

We lived in a house on land
from which the topsoil

had been removed. Wasps
fell into our shoes and

a blue light struck bacteria
dead in our water. Flight paths

followed the Hudson. At night, deer
crept from a wall of trees

to stand close to the house,
jaws moving. Three marriages

had unraveled there, the end
of one story beginning another.

We often traveled to mountains.
At Kaaterskill Falls, no signs

warned of danger, although
people sometimes died posing

for photographs, slipping backward
from the edge of wet rocks.

We tried hard to learn
the habits of hope.

We kept the hummingbird
that had impaled its body

high in the porch screen.
If our lights flickered

from time to time, we still
trusted them, even as

the night calmed its breath
and seemed to be lying

in wait. Inside, frost stretched
its roots through lungs

while the cats scattered
haphazard through winter-

chilled rooms, the fire
not yet lit. From time to time,

lion roars disturbed our sleep,
carried from the game farm

across the valley's swoop
by wind off the foothills.

We painted the house's high walls
while fog gathered between

window panes. The cats
stood by as birds

collided with glass, then lay still
in the yellow grass below.

Entering the Prayer

Something about shallows
and light pearling
in the collection units.

Our third month of catching
sleep in the cracks between.
And by catching I mean

as if a cat sliding
through one's fingers, all bent
bone and sinew. The girls

who ask to be *closer to God*
find themselves paralyzed,
drawing animals with teeth.

Birds come in for a landing
like a band of drummers.
Brick-dust sky.

The still center of the labyrinth.
We're at our wits' end
with yearning. The box

of the present, the cage of
the everyday. The body's
dumb ship navigating.

Marooned on the bed,
moon snarled in the branches
of the sugar maple.

Finch

The beached whale is shaped exactly like the house finch
whose body the dog has carried to the back door, gently,
placing it near the mat. Scientists do not know why
whales have lately begun emerging from the surf, their
bodies belly-up on the sand, except that collisions with a
ship seem likely. Meanwhile, our child wants to know
which items are edible in the video game he is playing.
"Can I eat broken eyeglasses?" he asks. He shows how his
character grimaces when it swallows sap, turns briefly
green with a cloud of gas emerging from its head. When
you call to say you'll be late, I am roasting vegetables on a
metal tray, kitchen windows steaming up in the half-light.
You will not say more about what you saw: a human body
along the highway, having stepped into traffic, choosing a
time and manner of death, cars backed up for miles.

+ + +

All night the dog asks to go out and then out again. She
seems to be trying to understand what it means to have
held the body lightly between her teeth, teeth sinking into
feathers and touching skin under which the heart once
thrummed like an insect beating its wings. I have risen
into wakefulness, not quite full alert but something else,
senses ringing as if from being struck and the sound
continuing on, like a bell, below the threshold of hearing.
It is that time again: the hour of night that brings with it

comfort, as if the dark placed its hands on us. "Is it possible he was all right?" I had asked. And you turned away, instead crying out from within sleep—*no, no, no*. Something has changed, but we have not learned what. The finch's wiry feet, her striated feathers, her beak like the hull of a boat.

In Which I See Your Double Coming

Suspended between two disbeliefs, I wait
for instructions to arrive, the letter to tell me
what needs to be done. I wasn't lying when I said
we can't return for the stinging nettles.
They're good for many things but so are
the plants I've found here along the tracks.
It still smells like a fire when we go outside,
but there's nothing that we can do about it.
Cameras stay trained in all four directions,
just in case. Toward morning, I dream of putting
one bullet after another into the bathroom wall
as shadows resume their steady march. I know
it sounds crazy, but I've sold my last regret,
auctioned it off to the highest bidder.
It's weapons-grade, if you're asking.

Portent

The meteor throws its weight against the atmosphere. *As if someone lit magnesium on fire, only brighter than any day you have ever seen.* There is not yet a name for this. Across five states, people come out of their houses to stare. *I thought a transformer blew,* one says. *I didn't worry.* The police lines are deluged with calls. They have nothing to say in return. Reports come in of babies arriving early, cows that cannot be righted, a mouse with two heads. The good news is the dog comes home again: a little worse for the wear, bedraggled and somewhat apologetic although her tail cannot stop wagging.

[this side of storm]

and if some failed to perceive
the day gone suddenly, shiftingly dark,
the river with its currents, this ground of
the beforelife, then I was the author of
my own buried longing,

horseweeds tall as our shoulders beaming
a last transmission, a rift widening between before
and now: and if the drone lifted into

another version of our lives, then at full blast
the hooves: life easier with a divine fate
but only metaphorically speaking,

a messenger bringing one to the end
of, as they say, the wheel: and who will gentle
the breath back into the dog?

in the beginning it was her heartbeat steadying mine,

diplopia, double vision, this side of
storm shearing branches from the Norway
maple so that when I turn on
the broad sway of landscape

air shimmers with halflife, as if giving us
everything in advance: stone foundations

where once a window and then wind
settling as if onto a couch, the
light to see objects by returning

it's true that no others again would be
better off than we were, sweat down our necks,
unmown grass, crepuscular: the house standing
then disappearing, names overwritten

the last time a way in or out, our shadows
thrown over the cliff's edge and
tables set for a crowd.

Miracle Town

in which the cage of the everyday opens

The trees really are coming alive, someone says on the bus. It is the way they thrash not only the tips of the branches but the roots as well, the way roots are beginning to tear up the sidewalks at the edges, living flesh snaking through concrete and dividing the small particles of rock. At night one can observe trees making their way through the neighborhood — maples and lilacs, the one last ash — leaves flapping like tongues as they congregate in small packs before dispersing and slipping back into the long pockets they have left in the soil. By morning it seems nothing has changed. Only the air through which the trees passed thrums at the seams as passersby thread toward their destinations. *I can do this,* one thinks. Another recognizes that the results resting in an envelope on the bureau are a door standing open. That she is still, at her core, a phoenix rising.

Evening, June

Glazed in lamplight—
air lifting the fern's arms,
lifting them into shadow.

Afternoon colored
the orange of your inner
eyelids, sleep-strewn.

Our rapid submersion
into summer, the sign's
shadow skating

the sidewalk, becoming
rooted to cement. Say:
I'm so good these days,

you wouldn't recognize
me. Hear: these days,
your hands, this bitter

earth. And think: the city.
Think: the painted shadows.
Air thin as tissue. Skin.

3.

Playground

We are seeing what happens
if we pretend the house ends

at the second door. It is
the day before the shutdown,

the last day, and I am sitting
waiting for my son

to exit the elementary. Everything
seems ordinary: the arches

of the playground equipment
blue and yellow, the knobs

on the trunk of the spiked evergreen
in the middle of the schoolyard.

The children wait at the structures
shaped like "N" and "O"

and there's no recourse
from what comes our way, only

shifts in the current that passes by.
The river moves in one direction

as does the line of cars. A week ago
I dug through the items in the lost

and found bin, where a family
of mice may have been living,

in search of my son's second boot,
which eventually turned up

on the front porch anyway. The sky
is a field of galloping horses, tails

streaming behind. When we pass
the roadside memorial, my son asks,

Did someone die here? and
truth be told there is no place

where someone or something
has not met an end. Yet the earth

keeps turning over, revealing
its soft underside. Turning in to

and out of darkness, the fine grains
of its accumulated soil coming

to surface, then doing
that for which they were made.

And just as the cupped funnel
on the playground reveals

the whisper at its other end,
we hear approaching hoofbeats.

The ground reverberates, as do
the small bones of our inner ears.

Homesteading

The thing with sleep is: I cannot recall
my last good one. During the second war

they stopped tracking those who jumped
from the bridge, who, it is said,

always faced the city with its ream of lights.
We invent ways to survive, knuckles

raw from washing, palms sore
from holding slogans. One by one,

the bannister spindles. Sleep the last refuge.
The northern latitudes pin us down.

I call to see if you've gone to the basement.
I build a secret place for our older child.

It is the blankets of my eyelids
that I covet most.

I shop for bread alone.
I inhabit my fears, also alone.

When I lock the door it means
the heart is a tender piece of meat.

I wake up and what more is there to say.
They are running to see if I am all right.

Death a woman bearing
a bouquet of flowers.

We sleep, one to each room,
because we can. The dull warmth

of the cat pressed to my side at night.
The muffled hum of the furnace.

Open House

/

The house begins to feel like someone else's long before we leave it. We box up our possessions, shift them aside for the cameraman who promises to show our rooms in their best light. And when a colony of flies erupts from the potatoes on the basement stairs two days before the open house, we hang strips of sticky paper — party streamers, the children call them — from the kitchen ceiling and keep going. A weekend away, we promise ourselves, will be just what we need.

//

At the place we've rented, we walk a gauntlet of wasps — we count two hundred — brought to life by September sun on the screened-in porch. Inside the upper rooms, one knocks its body against the skylight over and over as the dog walks through her own shit and lays a trail of pawprints across the white carpet. We spend the day at a decaying science museum filled with slightly dangerous machines that lift one's hair with electricity or permit one to cross a tightrope on a bicycle kept in place by a dangling counterweight. The children, both dressed in blue, demand our attention.

///

Later, we pick our way through tussock grass to feed some goats as the call comes in notifying us of a beginning—or is it ending? The children, buckled into their car seats, wait. When the wasps settle for the evening, we flee, the road's ribbon unfurling through darkened fields and evergreens in neatly planted rows. The city unfolds to greet us. Across its expanse, someone locks our house's door. Meanwhile, at the bottom of the trash can outside, a thick skein of fly strips lies hidden from view, some of the bodies still moving.

Finding a New Way Out

The wallpaper crawls
with scarabs.

When darkness takes on
the quality of cloth

and baffles sound,
my heart takes on water.

Salt spray lashes
rocks where birds

settle. The back of my hand
yellowed like paper

from an injury that arrived
without discernible source.

I take medicine
that dissolves sharp

on the tongue.
It is next week, and

already you are leaving.
The air this time of year

ridged with danger. Often
I wish for more light

than what's at hand.
Heart curled like a fox.

They say there is
displacement, there is

loss and, just like that, clouds
pile up on the horizon as

headlights sweep
the intersections.

The city's hive
beyond the dark room

filled with vending
machines. Is it right

that we sit eating together
under light that has taken

generations to reach us?
That we have chosen

our place beneath stars
that have collapsed already?

In Which We Set Aside Our Grievances

In the thick of it: summer furred and languorous.
I keep to the house. It's a fine day for spinning
a tale, a day packed with a hundred repetitions.
The wheat with its million thin strands. Let's not forget
how we once gathered the stems together, set them
in a tinted glass. All day I've been dreaming
of a room lit by soft white umbrellas. The house,
the listing said, would come equipped with everything
we might need, would give us a place to ride it out.
To admit this is no shortcoming. Please don't give
another thought to these matters. We must
advance our own interests, throw out
the baby with the bathwater.

The Sheep, in Wool Coats,
Did Not Suffer

While my daughter slept, I watched.
The day fit like a glove.
We sensed the way to make an opening was to tear.
Glass slippers grew in the field that year.
The best way to catch a mouse is by begging.
Glimpsed strands at times become a braid.
Some things only a woman will say.
Teach a cat to follow, and it will sit for hours.
The radiator's ribs the warmest place.
My daughter settled, muttering.
Her wings drew a shroud around her.
It is not usual for a child to grow wings.
Hers were like baby teeth: new and faintly dangerous.
It was a decade tinged with ice.
They talked of spreading plastic on the glaciers.
Water drained through ceiling lights.
The water we caught in cereal bowls, the mouse in a trap.
Its little skull just crushed in, she said.
Lunch always a sandwich, applesauce, and milk.
My daughter always cold.
She remembers darkness beyond the sliding door.
Not finding our shoes in the snow.
Shadows hunched behind bushes, indifferent.
The eyeless sky blank and shivering.

The Owls Come Calling

1.

A black grip, and absence watches.
Days convene their small red hatchmarks on the wall.
We wait in the wings of the city
for the act to unwrap itself.
       Trees prepare their branches.

       Time passes and yet.
Geese scissor their way across the sky, wedge after wedge.
       The parking lot is a sea of metal where
       people line up for "world-famous ice cream."
The sky has a mean look.

2.

It isn't the first time we've slipped back—
sticking to the edges of the streetpooled light.
       I seek a Morse code for my afflictions,
though gestures, it's true, are never enough.
       Some have the luck of being in the wrong place
       at the wrong time. Others, like me, carry

       a vague fog of disinformation into a room.
       What were you saying again? Have we met before?
Declare your intent and your fruit at the border.
A sound like the striking of a match.

The sound of laundry snapping in wind.
Behind: a line waiting. Before you: hills.

3.

Let's face it: the river, that is. And our lady who stands
        atop the bluff. The sunset cut
        from its moorings, colors sneaking off
        before we can stop them.

There's no harm in a promenade this time of night
        when people head west with their dogs.

        It's not the worst of all possible worlds.
The moon's fingernail scrapes its way
across the chalkboard, scripting sleep, footsteps, etc.
Behind you: waiting. Before: the night's slim hitch.

4.

Don't leave, someone says in the salt cave
of the hall. The night's breath
moves desire down your spine. You're sick with it.
It's getting almost time for the rivulets to come
        knocking, to muster a force that can take

the ice under, knuckle aside the crust of leaves that clogs
        the entrances and exits.
        Light shoves aside the curtain. The bed
        is a sickroom, walls dizzy gray

in the pallid afternoon. Ice cracks; the lake
once again shows its face. Last night the dog
crossed the street again: a black dog. Need you ask?

Some Brink

Disembarking, the man slings
a fish overshoulder as sun

lodged on its scales crazes
into silver ministrations.

This day a mouth; the day after, what?
I need someone to get drunk with,

you say. We sit in a café eating
fries from a cone of waxed paper.

The fish in a chair beside us.
Day hazed and ravenous.

Your cells have begun
their slow unraveling, though

we do not yet know it.
On our table, envelopes

stand at attention: gaping jaws.
In the next moment, glasses

leap from the shelves.
Buildings loom indecent

as the machine tears holes,
renders whole rooms visible.

And what descends
amid the snapping?

The shuffling off of skins?
The past claps its shutter closed

behind us. I take
the long way home, heels tapping.

Knight of Wands

Today the birthday piñata will fulfill the purpose for which it was made. We have sliced a hole in its outer surface through which we are inserting candy in metallic wrappers.

Soon the surgeon will do the same for my child, whose birthday it is, fashioning him a new ligament from his own body—an autograft, they call this—and stitch the torn parts that can be salvaged back together, removing what cannot be saved.

Eleven years ago walking in sun, the birth pains clenching my body. A new morning into which a new life would make itself known. A day marked by eclipse.

Today, waking into light filtered by the silver maple. We wished for a home surrounded by trees, and here we are.

The birthday piñata has four red legs supporting its body, a white face with an upturned nose and enormous, ridiculous ears that look like blue pompoms. Eyes that startled me two nights ago, coming up the stairs in the dark.

There is this body knitted within my own. We were two-hearted together for a while. I ferried him through the world. And then his body kept growing, its height nearly reaching my own. His knees with their four crucial ligaments holding strong for ten years. His right knee now with its trinity, its triumvirate.

This year I will entrust my child to a range of healers. They will teach him, but I will be the one there when he cries out in pain at what healing requires.

My heart settles itself in my chest, scrabbling out a nest in which to hide, to tend its wounds.

Crutches tap their way through the kitchen, the closing door. The surgeon will retract the skin gently, inserting the tools that will allow her space to maneuver. How long will it take, I asked. Just as labor fired up its engines and kept going.

It's only morning for a while, the sun already resecting its beams from the room.

We did not know this was what love would require. The piñata's tissue paper fur feathers in the moving air.

In Which the Season Turns on Its Hinge

Mist cloaks the window at night. Deer tracks
straddle the fencerows and keep on moving. We try
to remake ourselves into people who no longer
carry watches or phones. Who heed messages left
on lampposts, on bus station walls. Who know better
than to venture outside. I can't bear the way
everything holds still between two desires. Nothing
gates off the past from the future and, because of this, we traffic
in gestures instead of words. I can make neither heads nor tails
sprout from the prototypes. Which, unliving, continue
to stare from the borders of the room, the region beyond
the lamplight. The furniture, too, stands at attention.
I box up things only to find them again later. It's true
the signs have been there all along. Do you want me
to make something of them? Assemble the pieces and show
the image lurking on the other side? The world
transmogrified. Otherwise there's not much to do
but stock up on essentials: bread, milk, coffee.

The Fourth, Again

Already there are people planning
for the next days. And will it go on?

That's what no one can answer.

The air split with fireworks, their reverberations,
the creatures sent skittering for shelter.

We hunch in our room together, not

soundproof but muffled. There are
no headphones built for a dog, the dog

feeling the air's shimmy and hum in

the bright sounds shivering her skin.
Reverberations constant in the body

that I cannot wrap in comfort, only

place a pink pill far back in her throat
so that she can't help but swallow it,

then another half: split, crumpling

at the cut edge. Elsewhere, the sky shifts
in the same way, for the same reasons.

It's no good to wish things otherwise.

We are safe here for now, even though
purple sparks fountain upward

from the street outside our window.

Miracle Town

in which we count ourselves lucky

They finished the time machine on a Friday, ahead of schedule. The messages to gather had gone out, but by the time everyone convened, bearing platters heaped with steaming meat and casserole dishes weeping cheese, they were gone. No point in waiting, they said. Time to save the world. There was, at that time, a general consensus that things were going badly. The boy who hid himself at the edge of the clearing said that the machine folded into itself. Or that the edges grew dim, the bulk of the machine transparent. Later, the crowd could agree on very little, except for the sound, which was like glass breaking in a small room. We do not know if they succeeded in their mission. The fact that we are still here speaks volumes. We wash the dishes each night, sink into our slightly concave mattresses when the words on the page begin to swim past each other like errant minnows. Murmur to one another, *May _____ save you for another day*, though what we mean by this is, *May the swift horse of the week carry you past the next crossroads*. We could be forgiven for thinking that we'd have more time.

Surveillance: The River

In the flickering silence of the car, I want
to tell you. That darkness flowers

like a kind of distance. Rain: whose hands comb
the birches' many-stranded limbs. What transpires

cannot be named. The months keep flowing
in a timelessness that no longer bears

our imprint. Or the space we now inhabit.
Or inhabits us. Which is it? A seamlessness

has taken hold, got its claws into
the flesh of the day, the day that has given

ice back to the river. Wait. I want
to give this name: *gray transience* or *less than*

illumination. The green neon hush of grass
stakes out its claim. What bird of sadness

comes? Rhubarb-pink variations in the low-
flowering trees and, suddenly capsized,

the day's boat sinks without a ripple.
A certain, improbable light keeps shining.

4.

Looking Back, September

This time of year
the pooled light spilling.

We were afraid.

A world of
turning to feed and be fed.
Of saline hung in bags.

Knowing now
what I know, I would never.

That last morning
she did not move from the bed.
At which time we carried
her to the hospital.

All that goes into preparing
is not enough.

She died while receiving
an X-ray. Which later gave
information. Which showed
a tumor pressing on her lungs.

What passes for knowledge.

I still remember
the body laid upstairs and
entertaining a stranger in the kitchen.
We put all that aside for.

The fact is, I have shredded
the records, erased all evidence
of her passing.

Do not claim you are sorry.

I kept returning to the body
to see if breath
was lifting the ribcage, to find out
if some mistake had been made.

By which I mean

sun and how it
broke into white slats
on the floor.

Rabble

Breath slips easy from the lungs.

To cast off one habit is to take on another.
Buckling your seatbelt is one way to stay safe.

We base our interactions on a filial understanding.
Sound buckles the air, throws it up into ripples.
Put your head to the ground to hear approaching hoofbeats.

Their cadence shakes the thin bones in your ear: hammer, anvil, stirrup.
The proper names forgotten and no way to tell.
The column of cloud from its surroundings.
Scarcely had the doorbell rung than chaos descended.

Nothing can stand between a speeding car and its target.
I have not bones enough for this journey.
The maps trace out various routes that all end in conflagration.
The trees have been cut for their own good.
Buildings taken down brick by brick in no particular kind of order.

Slipping a peach into water before skinning is called scalding.
That movement is called a bonequake.
We sit in our usual places; you can't hold that against us.
It's true that I think of you often.
I wake with bruises that cannot be explained.

I re-lied, as in: I told you a different version of the truth.
There's no use grandstanding when no one is present to lend an ear.

We held a tea party under water before surfacing.
Bones awash in a silvered flash.

Safety in numbers can no longer be depended upon.
We called it a coup: the taking of the stands.
There is no blueprint for this unsettlement.

The featureless landscape.
This is not the time or the place for.

Each peach in its fragile jacket.

In Which I Am Not Sorry

A good detective begins by dusting for fingerprints.
We return home to find the door knocked in
like a tooth, the cats cowering under the bed.
The investigation is thorough, uncovering only
a smudge of lips on the glass's rim. We'd been advised
to photograph our possessions, make a list of all
we stood to lose. Spring comes and goes
with its sweep of birds: wings drumming across
the skyways, south to north. Now, we ache for things
to be different. Also for sleep to settle its feet
on our backs. The day's horoscope says, *You've been walking*
the straight and narrow too long. At the five-way
intersection, sirens tear the air. Streetlights like bells
in darkness. If you say "Truth be told," it means
the rest of the time you are withholding information.
You can't undo the future that calls you into being.
If you asked me, I'd say yes. What I will remember most
from that time: the hills that did not move an inch.

Miracle Town

in which our secret names come to light

No one notices the mirror on the far wall of the ice cream parlor, which is to say that they are distracted by the array of flavors to tempt the palate: Hungarian Double-Chocolate Success, Cheese and Coconut Soufflé with Reduction of Regret, and today's special: Winged Pomegranate Deluxe. The mirror is a thick slab, taller than a human, which reflects streamers hung from ceiling trusses, the groups huddled around small white tables and paper birds flitting from strings along the room's perimeter. The mirror is a door that does not open. Except once, a child observed the mirror's edge lifting off the wall, a hand extending to wipe a trace of syrup from her face before slipping back into nothing. She did not tell her mother. Instead, each time they come back for a cone of Strawberry Superhero, she finds herself unable to look away. Seeing only the grave face of herself framed by dark hair but imagining the tunnel that opens behind the mirror, the one that leads to the world in which her brother, who is not yet born, will fly a kite with her in a field of tossing wildflowers, their feet tangling in the stems, the kite descending like a stunned bird.

Halloween, 2016

The parade stretched for blocks through the neighborhood
where people stood holding trays of chocolate skulls.
A hunched-over bear raised its head in warning.

One by one lights came on, casting pools into which ambled
dinosaurs, superheroes in trailing capes, a stroller with its pumpkin
baby. We walked up hills for miles: no way to gauge our progress,

no pattern to our marching. We waded into the currents of
that river without flinching as evening slipped its hood over us.
We went as sheep calling to each other in the half-light.

Do not hold us accountable, the soles of our feet falling on
tracks left by mother and fathers, children that even
saints would not call from the crowd.

Dogs, too, walked among us. At that time some left
bowls on their front steps, though we couldn't be sure who watched
from between curtain panels. As the parade dissembled, figures melted

into shadow, faces blurred. At the block's end, someone
split wood, the air ringing in alarm. Soon, we were the only ones
moving between all those houses. I counted chimneys.

What force moved us along the sidewalks? We held hands
to avoid being separated as night drove its wedges between us.
It's true we did not have much farther to go.

Spooked

The paperwhites, growing
from their gold plastic bucket
in the middle of the table,
are not spooked.

The dog, lounging
in the brown chair, her head
draped over a pillow,
is not spooked.

The birds, engaged
in their daily emptying
of the feeder, continue.

The paper waits
to be written upon.
The spices in the kitchen
rest in their glass houses.

And we, who cannot set
our minds at ease, place feet
on the floor next to the bed,

pausing to let the day's weight
slide over our heads
like a turtleneck sweater.

We, who are caught up
in the day's news already,
pause before rising.

Already in the kitchen
the children call out, spoons
ringing against each other
as they exit the drawer.

Election Eve

In this year they are calling the darkest of timelines, I snap off
the lamp at the edge of my sons' room. Onscreen someone

is again calling for change, the night sky alight with words,
blooming with unseasonal warmth. The layered cloth

with which we guard our lungs insubstantial, scarcely enough
when I can sense the stars arrayed against us beyond stadium lights.

There's a certain tiredness to it all—a raggedness, as if
the year had done more than age us in its stripping away of

chances, lives, ceremonies on which we stood. What is left?
The sweet stench of leaves crumbling underfoot, the unbroken

moon. And more. We still have vegetables laid by, apples to fit
into brown paper jackets for storage. Whether it's all enough

remains to be seen. And yet. Here's the flush of evening
on the horizon, the trees standing guard, a little taller each year.

Why I Do Not Want a Christmas Tree

Because the snarl of packages inside our front door cannot be moved.

Because a great stuckness has taken root in our marriage and I do not know whether we will survive it.

Because I can't bear something else dying before my eyes. Because from the basement with my own hands I have removed their bodies.

Because I wanted our place to be a place of refuge and instead it has become a place of death. Because when I drew up a net of safety around us, I did not know that I would be required to place bait at intervals around the perimeter.

Because the mice which are now dying visited death on the baby songbirds growing in their high house this summer, and I was the one to find their bodies, heads gnawed open, on the steps below.

Because I buried the birds under the yew where none could find them.

Because the mouse who raised its head from the darkness of the birdhouse when I flicked on the porchlight showed no remorse.

Because I could not bury the others because then what poisons they possessed would make their way back out into the world. Because even though it would take fifty of those mice to fell a predator the size of a cat, there are such animals.

The Drowned Gate That
the Body Resembles

Last night I dreamed of ice breaking up
where a river meets the coast,
and I want you to notice

how the fractured blocks slide
past each other, aqua water
visible in the ripped seams.

Also my son saying,
I want to walk into a fire someday
because it's too hard being a grownup,

and this morning what I need to know is
how much should I worry?
It's not like we can comprehend

what life looks like without
us in it—any one of us—
and in the dream my grandfather

in the room's corner laughing, as
he rarely did in life. *I thought*
the seagulls were marshmallows,

my son says, *or flying Styrofoam.*
The bridge arcing up and over land.
Light slicing its crossroads into the sky.

We ask for a mirror, we ask for a
miracle, tongues ready to receive, one eye
tipped to the turquoise bowl

overhead the way chickens freeze at
the hawk's body scratched into
the surface above them. Lately

my heart is brittle, subject to
cracks/cracking even in
the absence of quake. The fear being

you have done it all wrong. You are not
a city on a hill. Meanwhile
there is a child still swinging

under winter-tinged clouds dragging
their tatters across the lake
and that child is me.

In Which We Ride the Train
Ten Years Out

It is a bruised sort of afternoon. Rain slaps
the windows. Fog stretches between us
and the headlands, erases all evidence
of our passing. It was winter when we met.
We stayed still so long the milk began to separate.
The footprints of animals began to look human.
An animal cannot lie, you told me. I tell you
plumeria has no nectar, only scent to lure
the gypsy moths at night. Ghost blossoms.
Hard-pressed to know when the rain might quit
its yammering, schools of clouds desist and
disperse. Is it wrong to say I loved? The sea
has escaped its shoreline. You'd swear the light
emanated. I have written your name on the inside
of my wrist. Once there was no body between us.

Autograft

I can't remember in whose foot the filament
lodged, shearing its way through the skin.

Here is a picture so we don't get lost.
The house is ours again, the pain

under retreat. Whose leg opened under
the scalpel? Meanwhile the robin

builds her nest just outside our window,
while outside my friend's house a squirrel

sits gnawing on a bone: a single vertebrae
by the looks of it. The city has cleared

our rabbit's body from the cross-
walk. Likewise the deer close to the highway exit

who lay there in the heat for a week.
Did the deer have a child? Did a nest

of baby rabbits lie tucked in low grasses
or did the mower catch them when it took down

the plants in the water retention lot?
I did not get a chance this season

to collect the trash before it was shredded.
Meanwhile the child's skin knits itself back together.

Where the scalpel's quicksilver traced a path
through layers, exposing sinew and bone,

a new ligament rests in the trough where blood
will thread its roots through rerouted tissue.

Meanwhile the splinter has been removed
from the foot, leaving a jagged exit wound.

Meanwhile the robin adds mud and bits of
fluff to her nest in the burning bush.

In Which We Count the Weeks Backward

On the anniversary, a faint glaze hits
the trail: the season hinged with frost, weeds
latched into a feathered crust. We notice the squirrels
have learned to regrow their limbs, the raccoons
become quicker, experts at evading the headlights'
paired eyes spinning down the highway. The deer
get up from where they lay beside pavement, and
the birds that had hurled their small bodies headlong
into propellers or glass begin stretching their wings,
slowly at first and later, after the thin bones
of evening have broken apart, take to the sky again.
In the back field, the coyotes carry on with
their raucous party. We wish them well, then head back
inside where the double-paned windows remain clear.
Night fissures, then collapses. Change impends.
It is frivolous, you remind me, to order curtains.

Looking for Something Beautiful

Say to me: *it is not yet winter*.
You have everything, still.

In this silence, in the slow drip
of water from the faucet, dishes

lie untouched, like always, laundry
piles up in the room's corners

like discarded leaves. I ask
if you remember the year

the trees seemed to drift
without end. I saved yellow

ginkgo fans in a jar, and
when the fish finally died,

you put it in the freezer, as if
such things should be kept—

life, or what once was life—
to be commemorated, rejoined.

This year, I will sow the leaves
back into the soil, and wait

for something new to emerge,
come spring. Know this, my friend:

what you have will not be everything
but will be enough. *It is enough.*

Acknowledgments

I am grateful to the editors of the following publications in which these poems first appeared, some in different forms or with different titles:

Alligator Juniper: "On Edge as if Breaking"

Amsterdam Quarterly: "Portent"

Anti-: "In Which Our Best-Laid Plans Come to Nothing"

Beloit Poetry Journal: "In the Midst of Reading Ammons"

Birdfeast: "Looking Back, September"

Boxcar Poetry Review: "In Which We Count the Weeks Backward"

Columbia: "The Sheep, in Wool Coats, Did Not Suffer"

Diode Poetry Journal: "In Which I Am Not Sorry," "In Which I See Your Double Coming," "In Which We Ride the Train Ten Years Out"

The Dodge: "The Owls Come Calling"

Folio: "Evening, June"

Handsome: "House Above the Bottomlands"

Jellyfish: "Entering the Prayer," "In Which I Try to Bring Back the Dead"

Josephine Quarterly: "In Which the Season Turns on Its Hinge"

The Laurel Review: "Rabble"

Magma: "Some Brink"

Memorious: "A Dangerous Time, These Hours in the Night"

Mid-American Review: "Meanwhile"

Moon City Review: "Miracle Town" [in which we count ourselves lucky]

Permafrost Magazine: "Finding a New Way Out"

River Styx: "Playground"

Rogue Agent: "In Which We Get Bogged Down in Inessentials"

Salt Hill: "Miracle Town" [in which everything is cast aside], "Miracle Town" [in which we embrace the evidence]

Southeast Review: "Surveillance: The River"

SWWIM Every Day: "Why I Do Not Want a Christmas Tree"

Third Coast: "Annunciation"

"Brother André's Heart, Montreal" was published in *Making Poems: 40 Poems with Commentary by the Poets*, eds. Todd Davis and Erin Murphy (State University of New York Press, 2010).

"Miracle Town" [in which everything is cast aside] was reprinted in *New Poetry from the Midwest 2019*, eds. Rita Mae Reese and Hannah Stephenson (New American Press, 2019).

"Portent" was reprinted in the *Amsterdam Quarterly 2017 Yearbook.*

"In Which I Am Not Sorry," "In Which I See Your Double Coming," "In Which I Try to Bring Back the Dead," "In Which Our Best-Laid Plans Come to Nothing, "In Which We Count the Weeks Backward," and "In Which We Ride the Train Ten Years Out" appeared in *Not If But When*, a limited edition chapbook (Salt Hill, 2016).

For their generous insights and the ways they have shaped the poems in this collection, thanks to Cynthia Marie Hoffman, Nina Clements, Jennifer Fandel, Erin Rudzicka Trondson, Heather Swan, Stella Nelson, Jason Gray, Rebekah Denison Hewitt, Natasha Oladokun, Noreen McAuliffe, Lisa Hollenbach, Michelle Niemann, Rena Leinberger (the last poem is for you), and Trent Miller, always. For time and space in which to write, appreciation to Edenfred, the Anderson Center, and the cities of Washington DC, Boston, Hudson, and Madison. For believing in my work and bringing this book into being, deep and abiding gratitude to Diane Lockward and Terrapin Books. And for everything else, profound appreciation and much love to my family—none of this would have been possible without you.

About the Author

J. L. Conrad is the author of the full-length poetry collection *A Cartography of Birds* (Louisiana State University Press), and the chapbooks *Recovery*, winner of the 2022 Robert Phillips Chapbook Prize (Texas Review Press), *Not If But When*, winner of the third annual Dead Lake Chapbook Competition (Salt Hill), and *Species of Light*, a limited-edition artist's book carried out in collaboration with printmaker Sarah Noble. Her poems have appeared in *Pleiades, Sugar House Review, Beloit Poetry Journal, Jellyfish*, and elsewhere. She earned her MFA in creative writing from American University and PhD in English from the University of Wisconsin–Madison. A native of Ohio, she currently lives in Madison.

www.jlconrad.com

Printed in the USA
CPSIA information can be obtained
at www.ICGtesting.com
LVHW020553090324
773966LV00005B/124